Elizabeth Stuart Phelps Ward

A Lost Hero

Elizabeth Stuart Phelps Ward

A Lost Hero

ISBN/EAN: 9783337185626

Printed in Europe, USA, Canada, Australia, Japan

Cover: Foto ©ninafisch / pixelio.de

More available books at **www.hansebooks.com**

A LOST HERO

A LOST HERO.

A LOST HERO

BY

ELIZABETH STUART PHELPS WARD

AND

HERBERT D. WARD

ILLUSTRATED BY FRANK T. MERRILL

BOSTON
ROBERTS BROTHERS
1893

University Press:
JOHN WILSON AND SON, CAMBRIDGE, U.S.A.

LIST OF ILLUSTRATIONS.

	PAGE
A Lost Hero	*Frontispiece*
The Express from Columbia	11
The Enterprise of the Summerville Merchant	12
In the Group at the Station stood a white Boy	13
The Boy tested the Halter, and patted the Horse	15
Stray Goats and Mules gazed expectantly	17
An old Negro came up	19
He plodded slowly up the Track	21
Snapped his Halter, and broke away	23
He got down on his Hands and Knees and crawled	24
Birds seemed to sing through the Air	25
Had the End of the World come?	27
They ran	31
The pauper Dog	32
They were only Cows	33

8   *List of Illustrations.*

PAGE

RUN FOR 'T! RUN! 37

AS THEY CAME ABREAST OF THE SECOND LITTLE
    STATION 41

I SOLE FOR TWO THOUSAND DOLLARS ONCT . 43

THE RAGGED OLD ARM THAT FELLED IT DOWN 45

THE LITTLE ONE CLIMBED LIKE A MONKEY
    UPON A SHELF 47

THE OLD MAN SEIZED THE TORPEDOES . . 48

THIS COMFORTED THE LAD INCREDIBLY . . . 49

"I STUMP YE!" 53

THE STRONG, BLACK FIST WAS CLINCHED . . 55

HE LAID ONE TORPEDO ON EACH RAIL . . . 57

PAPÄ! PAPÄ! 62

A LITTLE HUDDLING FIGURE 63

THE LOCALITY WHERE THE TRAIN STOOD WAS
    EXAMINED THOROUGHLY 67

HAD THE CURIOSITY TO PICK UP THE RAGS . 72

FINIS 74

NOTE.

THE materials of heroism are everywhere; each day and all situations are full of them. The power to recognize them and the will to use them make the hero. He who saves life, no matter how obscure, how poor, how ignorant he may be, has a value which can never belong to the spiller of blood; and the crimson glories of war fade before the white honors of peace.

This little story, which was originally contributed to the "Youth's Companion," has sought to teach the young people of America something of the grandeur which waits upon a brave deed, and something of the beauty of supreme self-sacrifice.

E. S. P. W.

H. D. W.

A LOST HERO.

THE express from Columbia was due. It was almost nine o'clock on Tuesday night, the 31st of August, 1886. It had been a hot day, sultry toward night, and the loungers at the Summerville station were divided between pitying and envying their neighbors on the excursion train. In such weather, home seems either the most intolerable or the most comfortable place in the world.

It had not rained for six weeks, and South Carolina panted.

"THE ENTERPRISE OF THE SUMMER-
VILLE MERCHANT."

There was a larger crowd than usual at the little station to see the Columbia excursionists come in. The enterprise of the Summerville merchant who placarded the pine-trees of this forest village with legends to the effect that his ice-cream would be found "Opp. the depot," was well rewarded that scorching night. The streets thronged — if Summerville streets can ever be said to throng — with warm and thirsty loungers of both sexes and of every color. South Carolinians though they were, they objected to the heat of that day.

In the group at the station stood a white boy, about ten years old, — a neatly dressed, well-behaved little fellow, with an expression of crushing and delightful responsibility. He wandered

"IN THE GROUP AT THE STATION STOOD A WHITE BOY."

back and forth restlessly and proudly
from the track to a tree in the square,
where an old horse and wagon were
fastened with unnecessary security.
The boy tested the halter, and patted
the horse continually.

It was a very important thing to drive
two miles in the dark for one's father
and bring him home from the nine
o'clock express. Add to this situation
the excitement of an excursion, and
Donny de Mone felt that life lacked
nothing more to the position and the
dignity of manhood. Besides, Donny
was very fond of his father, and had not
seen him for two weeks.

Now, there was one curious thing
about this crowd which would have
been noticeable to a stranger, but had
not as yet attracted the attention of the

"THE BOY TESTED THE HALTER, AND PATTED THE HORSE."

residents. This was the extraordinary number of animals that seemed to be waiting for this train. One would have thought that half the dogs in the neighborhood had relatives coming from Columbia.

Stray goats and mules gazed expectantly up and down the track. Cats had followed their owners from the houses and betrayed their devotion by subdued squeals from under their masters' regardless heels. A brindle-brown pig wriggled its way among the crowd, grunting with persistent uneasiness;

"STRAY GOATS AND MULES GAZED EXPECTANTLY."

2

while a couple of wandering cows, un-
molested by the strangely restless dogs,
passed and repassed the railroad cross-
ing, bellowing monotonously. The
horses at the station exhibited curious
discomfort; and Donny de Mone's
venerable nag " Ben Bow " astonished
the community by pulling at his
halter.

While the boy stood valiantly holding
the bridle, an old Negro came up and
pulled his sleeve. He was a shabby old
Negro. His lean knees protruded
through his trousers, — a mass of
patches from under which the original
material, like the jackknife in the mental
philosophy problem, had wholly disappeared. It was especially noticeable
that tufts of white hair found their way
through the holes in his coon-skin cap.

Across his shoulder he carried a bundle knotted into an old red handkerchief with a polka spot.

"Say, boss, cud ye tell me whar a

"AN OLD NEGRO CAME UP."

poah niggah cud fine a bit o' kivered hay to sleep on, an' a moufful o' pone in de mauhnin? I'se footed it clean from Charleston. I'se gwine to Branchville whar my dahter, Juno Soo, is a dyin' ob fever. She ain't long foh dis wohl. I'se got money 'nuff foh de breffust."

He looked wistfully at the lad. Donny answered with the heartiness of a child who has been brought up to think of others.

" My father will tell you when he comes in. I expect him every minute. But why don't you go to Kittie's." He mentioned the name of a woman well known in Summerville for strong character and wise benevolence. " She lives up the track there. Anybody will show you. She'll help you; she's the best colored woman in town."

The old man turned away without answering. Perhaps he thought this a pleasant device on the boy's part to

"HE PLODDED SLOWLY UP THE TRACK."

get rid of him. Perhaps he meant to follow his counsel. Who can say? He plodded slowly up the track and disappeared in the darkness.

I.

NOW, while Donny stood holding Ben Bow by the bridle, the old horse reared, plunged violently, snapped his halter, and broke away.

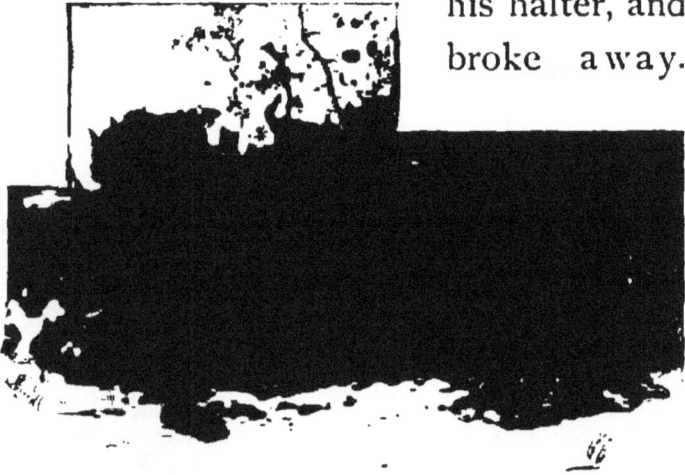

"SNAPPED HIS HALTER AND BROKE AWAY."

The boy, at the same instant, was hurled to the ground. The ringing of hoofs

and whir of wheels made strange sensa-
tions in his ears.   He thought what a
fool he was to be knocked down by old
Ben Bow.

Then he tottered to his feet.   Com-
plete darkness had come.   There was
an unearthly
silence.   Then
a moan, then
a howl and a
shriek arose
which reached
from group to
group, from
house to house,

"HE GOT DOWN ON HIS HANDS AND
KNEES AND CRAWLED."

from square to forest.   Human and
animal cries blended in one piteous
appeal for mercy.

Again the unknown power smote the
lad to the earth, which had become

"BIRDS SEEMED TO SING THROUGH THE AIR."

a raging sea. It rocked — it rolled.
Terrified, the child no longer attempted
to stand. He got down on his hands
and knees and crawled.

The trees whistled overhead. Flocks
of birds seemed to sing through the air,

striking against the telegraph wires.
The atmosphere, which but a few mo-
ments ago reeked with heat, took on a
grave-like chill. Again the earth heaved
and swayed beneath the frightened
youngster, who fell upon his face, vainly
clawing the ground for the support
which it denied him.

The station was only twenty yards
away. There, all the people were in a
turmoil. While endeavoring to regain
their feet, some were violently thrown
upon the wooden platform. Others,
holding to the side of the building, felt
with stupefaction the boards totter beneath their touch. Was judgment at
hand? Had the end of the world come?
The terror of a nameless danger unman-
ned the stoutest heart. Women shrieked
and prayed. Men cursed and groaned.

"HAD THE END OF THE WORLD COME?"

Donny had now joined the stricken group. They huddled together until another shock threw them one upon another. Delicate women became nauseated as if in mid-ocean. Sturdy men who had faced bullets in the Civil War without wincing, lost self-control. They surged; they fought; they comforted each other; they cried aloud.

At this moment a frightful tremor shook the earth. The station building gave sickening creaks; then it toppled with a crash.

Yell now followed yell. The crowd, that but now waited the joyous greetings of friends, was battered by the bruises of the earth and hurried by fright into a contagious state of mania. The bodies and faces of the people changed almost beyond recognition.

Maddened with fear, stunned by the last concussion, they stampeded.

The cry rang from mouth to mouth: " To the woods! To the hill! Home! Home!! Home!!!" They swayed; they rushed; they parted; they ran. Struck as by an invisible enemy, they fell prostrate in the powdery dust. They picked themselves up again and panted in their flight. A voice close to Donny's side rang above the uproar: " Good Lord! *It is an earthquake!* "

Like birds before a tornado, the people scattered to the right, to the left, — this way, that, and were gone. Donny found himself, dazed and alone, upon the cross-ties, groping toward the on-coming train. He thrust out his hands and stood a moment piteously crying, " Papä! Papä!" the most bewildered little fellow in all that frightened town.

To crawl up the track, to meet the train, to board her, to shriek at her,

"THEY RAN."

to get to his father, to cling to the cow-catcher, perhaps, till the engineer stopped for sheer

mercy, — this was the nearest approach
to a purpose that the child had, as he

beat along the track,
stumbling, falling,
up again, down
again, shaken by
the rolling earth,
and blinded by
darkness more aw-
ful than he had ever
seen or thought of.

A strange, thin
dog, without a col-
lar, whined at his
feet as he pushed
on, and licked his
hand and followed
him like his own.

"THE PAUPER DOG."

Huge, dim forms rushed alongside the
embankment, making unearthly sounds.

"THEY WERE ONLY COWS."

Dragons could not have seemed more dreadful; but they were only cows. Huge pine-trees bent to the earth with rapid, vibratory motion as if a giant's hand clutched and shook them by the roots.

All the time the awful rumbling of the earth went on; it sounded as if the world were turning herself over, and thrashing to and fro in a fit of anger; before every convulsion she uttered a roar which seemed as if it came from a metal ball bowled along a giant alley beneath. It reached its climax by trilling the letter *R-r-r-r!* in a mighty voice. Then came the shock.

Suddenly, as the child was making his way through the horror and desolation of this scene, he felt himself clasped in the outstretched arms of a figure hurrying from the opposite direction. The two came together in the dark with a jolt, and recoiled.

"Goramercy!" said a quavering voice. It was the speech of the old Negro track-walker, taking two days to get to his dying daughter because he could not afford the railroad ticket that would have brought him to her in two hours. Donny recognized the high, cracked, pathetic tones which had addressed him at the station.

" De track 's busted!" panted the Negro. " De rails is done gone twist wid de shakes. Dey lays like er heap ob corn-shuck in de win' up yander. Dat ar train don' know hit, an' she 'll go to Day ob Jedgment, an' ebery soul aboard ob her! I'se run like de nation fer to warn de town!"

"RUN FOR'T! RUN!"

"Oh, there is n't any town to warn!" cried Donny. "It 's all run off! There is n't anything left but the earthquake and me — and this pup — and nobody to do anything — and my papä 's aboard that train! Oh, what shall we do? What shall we do?"

"Run, honey, run!" said the old man, more hopefully. "Mebbe we 'll head her off some ways or 'nuther. Run for 't! Run!"

The dirty old black hand clasped the tender little white one, which nestled into it gratefully. What it meant at that awful time not to be alone, — to feel a human touch, to know that a human heart beat beside you, — one would have to be in the child's place to understand.

II.

THE two ran, plunging up the dis-
torted track which swelled and
shook beneath them, toward the com-

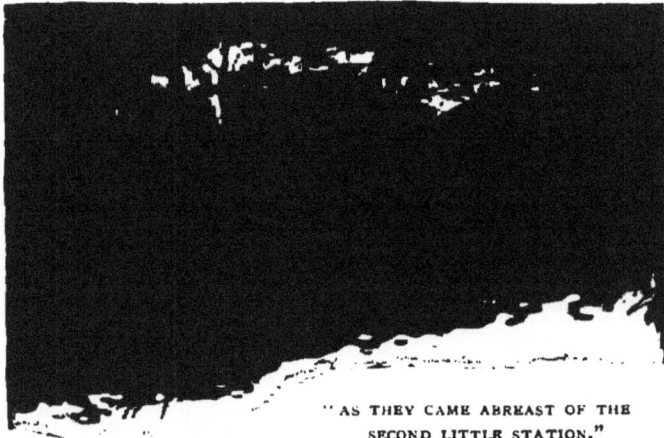

"AS THEY CAME ABREAST OF THE
SECOND LITTLE STATION."

ing train. As they came abreast of the
second little station, known as the

West End station of Summerville, an idea shot like hope itself through the confused brain of the hurrying boy.

"I know where the torpedoes are!" he cried, shrilly. "The torpedoes they put down to stop trains! I've seen 'em. I play with the superintendent's boys sometimes. If I was bigger I could bu'st open the doors and windows and find 'em."

"I'se an ole man," shouted the Negro, "but I'se been a tough one befo' Freedom. I sole for two thousand dollars onct. I kin smash 'most anythin' yer give me, honey, if hi'm put to't. If der's anythin' wantin' to be bu'sted to stop dat ar train, I reckon I kin bu'st."

Whirling along, in the dark and the uproar, the two panting figures rushed against the little station. It was very

"I SOLE FOR TWO THOUSAND DOLLARS ONCT."

dark. In a lull of the raging earth the distant whistle of the train could be distinctly heard.

"THE RAGGED OLD ARM THAT FELLED IT DOWN."

"In there!" cried the boy. "There! *There!* Oh, don't you think perhaps my papä took some *other* train? Oh, she's coming! I'll help. I can help. Oh, the door's too big for me!"

But not too big for the ragged old arm that felled it down as an axe fells the last rings of a stricken tree. Not too big for the remnant of strength in the once muscular slave. Not too big for the fiery old heart that trouble and toil and hunger and loneliness had never quenched.

The door went down — glass crashed — another door yielded — two wild figures fell into the superintendent's private office. The little one climbed like a monkey upon a shelf he knew of, and then the two rushed out of the rocking building into the resounding air, on which human shrieks smote steadily, as it was said they did all that awful night.

Again, the whistle of the train — near now — nearer —

As the pathetic couple ran up the torn and twisted track, Donny began to sob aloud ; but all he said was, "Papä! Papä! Papä!"

" Gib 'em to me, sonny," said the Negro, with the authority of age and danger. "I kin run faster 'n you, honey! Goramercy, *dar she am !*"

"THE LITTLE ONE CLIMBED LIKE A MONKEY UPON A SHELF."

The old man seized the torpedoes,
and rushing away with them, vanished
in the darkness.   The unknown, collar-

"THE OLD MAN SEIZED THE TORPEDOES."

less dog followed him.   Donny, sobbing
and calling his father's name, pushed on

as well as he could by himself. As he
ran he tried to say his prayers, but all

"THIS COMFORTED THE LAD INCREDIBLY."

he could remember was, " Our Father
who art in heaven."

Then he thought, how soon might
his father on earth be father in heaven,

4

too? He could not say that prayer. The boy, like many an older and wiser than Donny, only cried instead of praying. As he ran along in this sad fashion, something hit against him, whinnying in the dark. It was Ben Bow, the horse he had ridden ever since he was a baby. Now, this comforted the lad incredibly, to have one of the family with him.

III.

THE old man and the train were now face to face. The locomotive came cautiously, for the shocks had penetrated far up the road, but too fast — far too fast. Where the track had gone to pieces, a mass of twisted rails and tossing sleepers and furrowed earth, a bank — what is called a high bank in Southern topography — raised itself just in the turn of time to have sent the derailed train plunging down.

The old Negro watched the approaching flare of the head-light as he ran on, with a grim, defiant eye.

" I stump ye ! " he said aloud. He shook his trembling, black fist at the locomotive. Stumbling along, his old bundle over one shoulder, and the torpedoes clutched in the other arm, being thus encumbered — for it did not occur to him that he could throw away his bundle, he was so poor—he tripped and fell. His foot caught ; it is unknown in what, — in a twisted tie, or perhaps in a crevice of the cracking earth.

When he tried to rise, something held the hero down. He reached his whole length forward flat upon the road-bed, and with great precision and with a coolness that one cannot think of now without emotion, he laid one torpedo on each rail, exactly where it needs must lie to give the warning through the crushing wheel.

"I STUMP YE!"

Now for the second time the old man and the locomotive regarded each other. Her fiery breath was close upon him.

"THE STRONG, BLACK FIST WAS CLINCHED."

Above the uproar of the reeling earth the shriek of the train sounded in his

deafened ears.   Once again, the strong,
black fist was clinched in the approaching monster's face.

"I dare ye!" he cried.   "Come on!
I dare ye!"   He pulled himself up with
a mighty wrench.   But the unknown
power held him.   He felt the claws of
the cow-catcher.   He gave one low cry:

"Lord, I'd like to got dar an' seen
Juno Soo afore she died —"

Then he closed his eyes, that he
might not see what would happen,
clasped his hands above his gray head,
and gave his manly soul to God.

"HE LAID ONE TORPEDO ON EACH RAIL."

IV.

THE anxious and bewildered passengers heard the snap! snap! of the torpedoes, and half of them rushed to the platforms. The engineer signalled " Down brakes!" and the train, with a mighty jolt, came to a stop. A heavy shock shook the night at that instant. The smell of sulphur was strong in the chilly air. The engineer got out with a lantern. The crowd gathered in a moment. At the brink of the scattered track, at the very edge of wreck and death, the train had come to a stand.

"Who did it?" swept from lip to lip. No one was in sight.

" I thought we hit a man," said the engineer, swinging his lantern far out into the darkness. But no sign, whether of the dead or of the living, was in sight, — nothing except a half-starved, collarless dog, who sat stupidly upon the grass, and who did not even wag his tail when the stoker spoke to him.

" Who saved us? Who saved the train ? "

Ask the disappointed vulture and the mouth of the muttering earth to tell you, gentlemen passengers ! There is no other lip to answer.

Yes, there is one; a little, trembling, ashy lip — a child's — scarcely able to articulate for grief or terror, and pouring forth confused cries that nobody can understand. The passengers have left the train, and are making their way cautiously homeward down the devastated road-bed, where the track had lain. It is hurled now to every point of the compass in the wild night.

They come to a halt suddenly, before a little huddling figure, with its face hidden in its arms, crouched beside a crooked rail. An old horse, with traces hanging and harness a wreck, stands snorting beside the boy.

"Donny! Donny! Why, my sonny boy!"

The crowd parts for a thin, white-faced man, — the passenger who had been heard to say upon the way, "My little son is coming to meet me. I hope these shocks do not extend to the Summerville station."

There is one other little wild call, "Papä! Papä!"—a tremendous effort

to be manly, and not cry before strangers — and the boy melts into his
father's arms, and wonders whose tears
they are which
rain upon his
cuddling face.

But who saved
the train? Where
is he? How did
he do it? Who
took that noble
risk? Where is
the hero? Here?

"*You*, my lad?"

Then Donny
raised his awe-
struck face from

"PAPÄ! PAPÄ!"

his father's quick-beating heart, and
standing among the strangers and the
neighbors, told the story, — all that he
knew; all that he could tell.

"A LITTLE HUDDLING FIGURE."

" I only remembered the torpedoes, sir. The old man did the rest."

" What old man ? Where is he ? "

" Why, the old colored man! Haven't you seen him ? The old colored man who ran ahead and put them on the track. *He* saved the train."

The engineer took his lantern and silently went back and swung the spot of fire in the black, cold air. It had not rained, as we have said, for many weeks, but his feet splashed into deep pools and running rivulets, and sank into crevices and gashes in the trembling earth.

A few of the passengers followed the engineer. The locality where the train stood was examined thoroughly. Again, the same result,— no human creature, dead or living, was to be seen. The pauper dog sat just where they had left him. The engineer went up and patted him. At the touch he fell over — dead of fright.

They returned to report what they had found. As they did so, they called and shouted into the darkness, seeking for the brave life that had saved their own. Only the roar of the earthquake answered them.

" But he *must* be there ! " cried the lad, "of course he's there. He's a very shabby old Negro. He is all patches and his knees and hair stick out. His hat looked like a coon-skin hat. His hair is gray hair. He carries a little bundle on his shoulder. He's a very strong old Negro. He smashed the station in like — like blocks. He was a slave, and he was so strong he cost two

"THE LOCALITY WHERE THE TRAIN STOOD WAS EXAMINED
THOROUGHLY."

thousand dollars. He's going to see his daughter in Branchville. She's dying. He's so poor he had to walk from Charleston all the way. *He* saved the train. You just look and you'll find him."

A mighty shock drowned the boy's words at this moment, and seemed to jeer at them. The people huddled together, and looked into each others' appalled faces, and no man said a word. Instinctively they ranged themselves into a mass, as if united humanity could defy aroused and raging Nature, — then broke, and ran for their homes, and wives and babes, and whatever fate had left to them.

V.

BUT where is the hero? Who saved the train? Summerville, to this day, goes seeking him, and her search is a vain thing. Will he not break his long, mysterious silence? Will he not come forth to take the blessing of the grateful people? An obscure old Negro, poor, hungry, and homeless, will he not accept the proffered reward? Where is the hero?

Like Moses of old, hath God buried him? The earth knows, which yawned beside the track — and closed again — when the crushing wheels struck the life from the unknown savior of the excursion train. The earth knows; but she keeps her secret. Her awful lips are dumb.

"HAD THE CURIOSITY TO PICK UP THE RAGS."

Some weeks after the shock of August 31, a section hand, setting a sleeper, found an old bundle, soiled and wet, tied to a stick and mouldering in the ground. He opened it carelessly, and threw it away, and hardly thought to mention it to his overseer, who had the curiosity to pick up the rags and examine them.

A handkerchief, once red, with polka spots, contained a ragged flannel shirt and a stocking-heel tied with a piece of tape. That was all. This stocking-heel, evidently the wallet of some poor traveller, held one silver piece of the value of ten cents, two coppers, and a newspaper clipping, old and faded. It was a copy of the Proclamation of Emancipation to the Negro slaves of

America, beginning, " I, Abraham Lincoln," and bearing date Eighteen Hundred and Sixty-three.